MAKE IN A WEEKEND

Afghans to knit

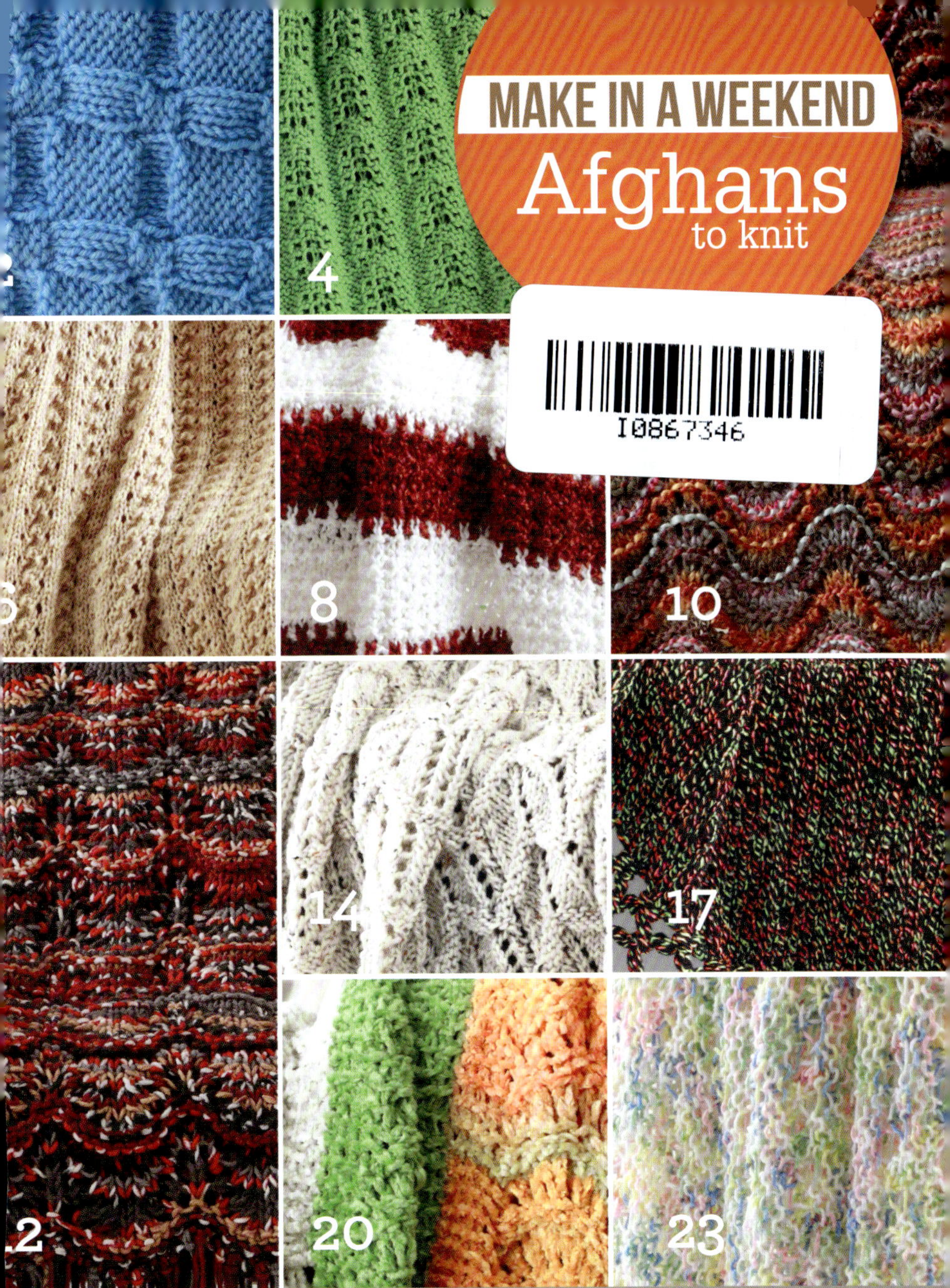

Start and finish an afghan in one weekend! It's easy with the 10 simple knit designs in this collection from Rita Weiss. Choose from baby wraps or jumbo throws for the family room.

LEISURE ARTS, INC.
Maumelle, Arkansas

Baby Boy Blue

Finished Size: 38" (96.5 cm) square

BEGINNER

SHOPPING LIST

Yarn (Medium Weight) MEDIUM 4

[3.5 ounces, 170 yards (100 grams, 150 meters) per skein]:

☐ 5 skeins

Knitting Needle

29" (74 cm) circular

☐ Size 11 (8 mm) **or** size needed for gauge

GAUGE INFORMATION

In Garter Stitch (knit every row), 12 sts = 3¾" (9 cm)

Note: Circular needle is used to accommodate large numbers of stitches. Do not join; work back and forth in rows.

AFGHAN

Cast on 122 sts.

Rows 1-6: Knit across.

Row 7: K 10, P3, ★ K6, P3; repeat from ★ across to last 10 sts, K 10.

Row 8: K4, P6, ★ K3, P6; repeat from ★ across to last 4 sts, K4.

Rows 9-14: Repeat Rows 7 and 8, 3 times.

Row 15: K4, P6, ★ K3, P6; repeat from ★ across to last 4 sts, K4.

Row 16: K 10, P3, ★ K6, P3; repeat from ★ across to last 10 sts, K 10.

Rows 17 and 18: Repeat Rows 15 and 16.

Repeat Rows 7-18 for pattern until piece measures approximately 37" (94 cm) from cast on edge, ending by working Row 13.

Last 6 Rows: Knit across.

Bind off all sts in **knit**.

Beautiful in Green Squared

Finished Size: 48" (122 cm) square

EASY

SHOPPING LIST

Yarn (Medium Weight) MEDIUM 4

[7 ounces, 364 yards
(198 grams, 333 meters)
per skein]:

☐ 4 skeins

Knitting Needle

36" (91.5 cm) circular

☐ Size 9 (5.5 mm)
or size needed for gauge

GAUGE INFORMATION

In Body pattern,
22 sts = 4¾" (12 cm)

TECHNIQUES USED

- YO *(Fig. 1a, page 27)*
- K2 tog *(Fig. 2, page 27)*
- SSK *(Figs. 5a-c, page 28)*

Note: Circular needle is used to accommodate large numbers of stitches. Do not join; work back and forth in rows.

AFGHAN

Cast on 222 sts.

Rows 1 and 2: Knit across.

Row 3 (Right side)**:** K1, ★ K2 tog twice, (YO, K1) 3 times, YO, SSK twice; repeat from ★ across to last st, K1.

Row 4: Purl across.

Rows 5-10: Repeat Rows 3 and 4, 3 times.

Rows 11-14: Knit across.

Repeat Rows 3-14 for pattern until piece measures approximately 48" (122 cm) from cast on edge, ending by working Row 13.

Bind off all sts in **knit**.

Lovely and Warm

Finished Size: 50" x 60" (127 cm x 152.5 cm)

EASY

SHOPPING LIST

Yarn (Medium Weight) MEDIUM 4
[7 ounces, 364 yards
(198 grams, 333 meters)
per skein]:

- ☐ 7 skeins

Knitting Needle
36" (91.5 cm) circular

- ☐ Size 10 (6 mm)
  or size needed for gauge

GAUGE INFORMATION

In pattern (Rows 6-9),
14 sts = 3" (7.5 cm)

TECHNIQUES USED

- YO *(Figs. 1a & b, page 27)*
- P3 tog *(Fig. 4, page 28)*

Note: Circular needle is used to accommodate large numbers of stitches. Do not join; work back and forth in rows.

AFGHAN

Cast on 234 sts.

Rows 1-5: Knit across.

Row 6 (Right side)**:** Knit across.

Row 7: K4, purl across to last 4 sts, K4.

Row 8: K6, YO, P1, P3 tog, P1, ★ YO, K2, YO, P1, P3 tog, P1; repeat from ★ across to last 6 sts, YO, K6.

Row 9: K4, purl across to last 4 sts, K4.

Repeat Rows 6-9 for pattern until piece measures approximately 59" (150 cm) from cast on edge, ending by working Row 9.

Last 5 Rows: Knit across.

Bind off all sts in **knit**.

Rhapsody in Red and White

Finished Size: 43" x 48" (109 cm x 122 cm)

EASY

SHOPPING LIST

Yarn (Bulky Weight) BULKY 5

[6 ounces, 185 yards (170 grams, 160 meters) per skein]:

- ☐ White - 4 skeins
- ☐ Red - 3 skeins

Knitting Needle

36" (91.5 cm) circular

- ☐ Size 11 (8 mm) **or** size needed for gauge

GAUGE INFORMATION

In pattern,12 sts = 4" (10 cm)

Note: Circular needle is used to accommodate large numbers of stitches. Do not join; work back and forth in rows.

AFGHAN

With White, cast on 129 sts.

Row 1 (Right side)**:** With White, K1, ★ with yarn in **back**, slip 1 as if to **purl**, K1; repeat from ★ across.

Row 2: K1, ★ with yarn in **front**, slip 1 as if to **purl**, K1; repeat from ★ across.

Rows 3 and 4: Knit across.

Rows 5-20: Repeat Rows 1-4, 4 times; at end of Row 20, cut White.

Rows 21-32: With Red, repeat Rows 1-4, 3 times; at end of Row 32, cut Red.

Rows 33-48: With White, repeat Rows 1-4, 4 times; at end of Row 48, cut White.

Rows 49-60: With Red, repeat Rows 1-4, 3 times; at end of Row 60, cut Red.

Rows 61-260: Repeat Rows 1-60, 3 times; then repeat Rows 1-20 once **more**; at end of Row 260, do **not** cut White.

Bind off all sts in **knit**.

Ripple Romance

Finished Size: 45" x 57" (114.5 cm x 145 cm)

EASY

SHOPPING LIST

Yarn (Medium Weight) MEDIUM 4

[3.5 ounces, 147 yards
(100 grams, 134 meters)
per skein]:

- ☐ 13 skeins

Knitting Needle

36" (91.5 cm) circular

- ☐ Size 9 (5.5 mm)
  or size needed for gauge

GAUGE INFORMATION

In pattern (Rows 6-9),
18 sts = 4" (10 cm)

TECHNIQUES USED

- YO *(Fig. 1a, page 27)*
- K2 tog *(Fig. 2, page 27)*

Note: Circular needle is used to accommodate large numbers of stitches. Do not join; work back and forth in rows.

AFGHAN

Cast on 216 sts.

Rows 1-5: Knit across.

Row 6 (Right side)**:** Knit across.

Row 7: Purl across.

Row 8: K2 tog 3 times, (YO, K1) 6 times, ★ K2 tog 6 times, (YO, K1) 6 times; repeat from ★ across to last 6 sts, K2 tog 3 times.

Row 9: Knit across.

Repeat Rows 6-9 for pattern until piece measures approximately 56" (142 cm) from cast on edge, ending by working Row 9.

Last 5 Rows: Knit across.

Bind off all sts in **knit**.

Warm as Toast

Finished Size: 36" x 60" (91.5 cm x 152.5 cm) excluding fringe

EASY

SHOPPING LIST

Yarn (Bulky Weight)

[3.5 ounces, 127 yards (100 grams, 116 meters) per skein]:

- ☐ 11 skeins

Knitting Needle

36" (91.5 cm) circular

- ☐ Size 13 (9 mm) **or** size needed for gauge

Additional Supplies

- ☐ Crochet hook (for fringe)

GAUGE INFORMATION

In Garter Stitch (knit each row), 10 sts = 4" (10 cm)

TECHNIQUES USED

- YO *(Fig. 1a, page 27)*
- K2 tog *(Fig. 2, page 27)*
- Slip 1, K1, PSSO *(Figs. 6a & b, page 29)*

Note: Circular needle is used to accommodate large numbers of stitches. Do not join; work back and forth in rows.

AFGHAN

Cast on 93 sts.

Rows 1-4: Knit across.

Row 5 (Right side)**:** K5, K2 tog twice, (YO, K1) 3 times, YO, (slip 1, K1, PSSO) twice, ★ K1, K2 tog twice, (YO, K1) 3 times, YO, (slip 1, K1, PSSO) twice; repeat from ★ across to last 5 sts, K5.

Row 6: K4, purl across to last 4 sts, K4.

Rows 7-12: Repeat Rows 5 and 6, 3 times.

Repeat Rows 1-12 for pattern until piece measures approximately 58" (147.5 cm) from cast on edge, ending by working Row 12.

Last 6 Rows: Knit across.

Bind off all sts in **knit**.

FRINGE

Holding one strand of yarn, 14" (35.5 cm) long, add fringe in each stitch across both short ends of Afghan *(Figs. 8a & b, page 30)*.

Fisherman Ripple

Finished Size: 46" x 50" (117 cm x127 cm) excluding fringe

EASY

SHOPPING LIST

Yarn (Medium Weight) MEDIUM 4
[5 ounces, 260 yards,
(141 grams, 238 meters)
per skein]:
- ☐ 8 skeins

Knitting Needle
36" (91.5 cm) circular
- ☐ Size 10½ (6.5 mm)
  or size needed for gauge

Additional Supplies
- ☐ Crochet hook (for fringe)

GAUGE INFORMATION
In Garter Stitch (knit every row),
14 sts = 4" (10 cm)

TECHNIQUES USED
- YO *(Fig. 1a, page 27)*
- K2 tog *(Fig. 2, page 27)*
- Slip 1 as if to **knit**, K1, PSSO *(Figs. 6a & b, page 29)*
- Slip 1 as if to **knit**, K2 tog, PSSO *(Fig. 7, page 29)*

Note: Circular needle is used to accommodate large numbers of stitches. Do not join; work back and forth in rows.

AFGHAN
Cast on 187 sts.

Rows 1 and 2: Knit across.

Row 3 (Right side)**:** K3, YO, K3, slip 1 as if to **knit**, K1, PSSO, YO, slip 1 as if to **knit**, K2 tog, PSSO, YO, K2 tog, K3, ★ YO, K1, YO, K3, slip 1 as if to **knit**, K1, PSSO, YO, slip 1 as if to **knit**, K2 tog, PSSO, YO, K2 tog, K3; repeat from ★ across to last 3 sts, YO, K3.

Row 4: K2, purl across to last 2 sts, K2.

Rows 5-11: Repeat Rows 3 and 4, 3 times; then repeat Row 3 once **more**.

Row 12: Knit across.

Instructions continued on page 16.

Row 13: K2, purl to last 2 sts, K2.

Row 14: Knit across.

Repeat Rows 3-14 until piece meaures approximately 50" (127 cm) from cast on edge, ending by working Row 12.

Last Row: Knit across.

Bind off all sts in **knit**.

FRINGE

Holding 10 strands of yarn, each 18" (45.5 cm) long, add fringe to sts at "points" and "valleys" across short edges of Afghan ***(Figs. 8a & b, page 30)***.

Midnight Magic

Finished Size: 40" x 54" (101.5 cm x 137 cm) excluding fringe

EASY

Instructions continued on page 18.

SHOPPING LIST

Yarn (Medium Weight) MEDIUM 4

[3.5 ounces, 179 yards
(100 grams, 163 meters)
per skein]:

- ☐ 7 skeins

Knitting Needle

36" (91.5 cm) circular

- ☐ Size 15 (10 mm)
  or size needed for gauge

Additional Supplies

- ☐ Crochet hook (for fringe)

GAUGE INFORMATION

In Stockinette Stitch
(knit 1 row, purl 1 row),
10 sts = 4" (10 cm)

Note: Circular needle is used to accommodate large numbers of stitches. Do not join; work back and forth in rows.

AFGHAN

Cast on 113 sts.

Row 1: K5, ★ slip 1 as if to **purl**, K5; repeat from ★ across.

Row 2: P5, ★ slip 1 as if to **purl**, P5; repeat from ★ across.

Row 3: K5, ★ slip 1 as if to **purl**, K5; repeat from ★ across.

Row 4: Purl across.

Repeat Rows 1-4 for pattern until piece measures approximately 54" (137 cm) from cast on edge, ending by working Row 4.

Bind off all sts in **knit**.

FRINGE

Using photo on page 17 as a guide for placement and holding 8 strands of yarn, each 25" (63.5 cm) long, add fringe to sts across short edges of Afghan ***(Figs. 8a & b, page 30)***.

Divide fringe into 4 strands and knot strands together approximately 1½" (4 cm) below cast on edge ***(Fig. A)***; repeat across.

Divide strands again and knot together approximately 1" (2.5 cm) below first knots, repeating across ***(Fig. B)***.

Fig. A

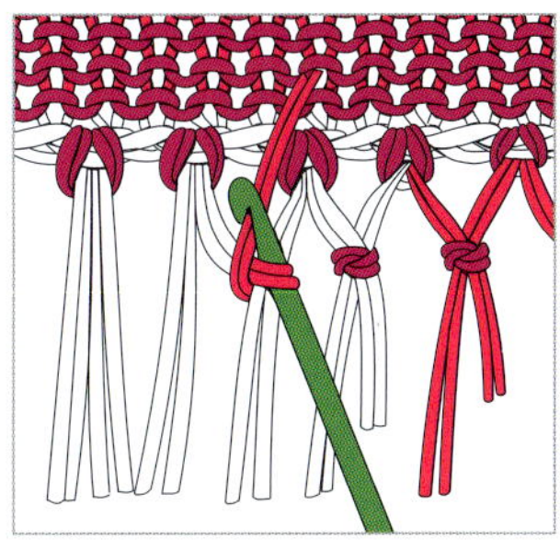

Fig. B

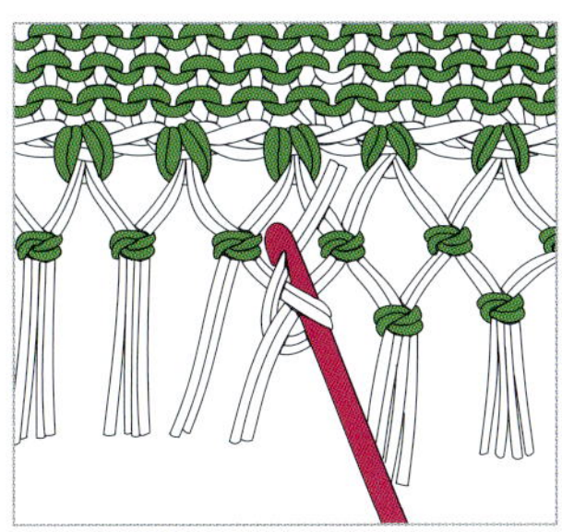

Simple Stripes

Finished Size: 58" x 54" (147.5 cm x 137 cm) excluding fringe

EASY

Note: Afghan is shown folded in half. The grey panel at left is the center of the afghan.

SHOPPING LIST

Yarn (Bulky Weight) BULKY 5
[2.5 ounces, 100 yards
(71 grams, 91 meters) per skein]:
- ☐ Grey - 6 skeins
- ☐ Green - 6 skeins
- ☐ Variegated - 6 skeins

Knitting Needle
36" (91.5 cm) circular
- ☐ Size 17 (12 mm)
  or size needed for gauge

Additional Supplies
- ☐ Yarn needle

GAUGE INFORMATION
In pattern (Rows 6-11),
8 sts = 5" (12.75 cm)

TECHNIQUES USED
- YO ***(Fig. 1a, page 27)***
- K2 tog ***(Fig. 2, page 27)***
- P2 tog ***(Fig. 3, page 28)***

Note: Circular needle is used to accommodate large numbers of stitches. Do not join; work back and forth in rows.

CENTER PANEL
(Make 2)

With Grey, cast on 16 sts.

Rows 1-5: Knit across.

Row 6 (Right side)**:** K4, YO twice ***(Fig. A)***, K1, (YO twice, K1) across to last 4 sts, YO, K4: 33 sts.

Fig. A

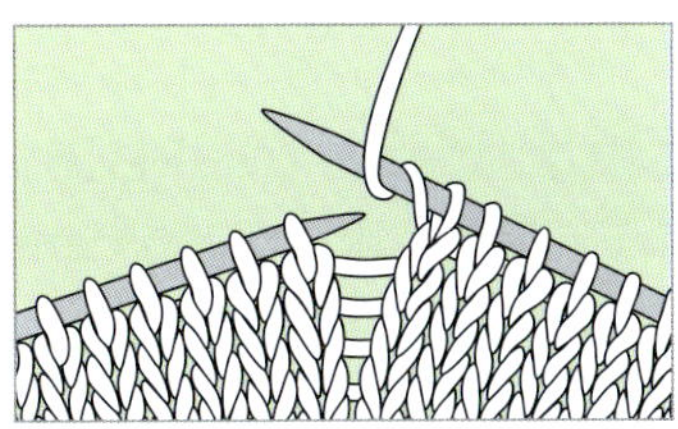

Row 7: K4, drop next YO from needle, ★ purl next 2 sts dropping one YO from needle; repeat from ★ across to last 4 sts, K4: 24 sts.

Instructions continued on page 22.

Rows 8 and 9: K4, K2 tog, knit across to last 6 sts, K2 tog, K4: 20 sts.

Row 10: K4, P2 tog, purl across to last 6 sts, P2 tog, K4: 18 sts.

Row 11: K4, K2 tog, knit across to last 6 sts, K2 tog, K4: 16 sts.

Repeat Rows 6-11 for pattern until piece measures approximately 58" (147.5 cm) from cast on edge, ending by working Row 11.

Last 8 Rows: Knit across.

Bind off all sts in **knit**.

SIDE PANEL (Make 2)

With Green, work same as Center Panel.

END PANEL (Make 2)

With Variegated, work same as Center Panel.

ASSEMBLY

Holding two grey Center Panels with **right** sides up and cast on edges together, sew long edges together ***(Fig. B)***.
Using photo on page 20 as a guide for placement, add green Side Panels and variegated End Panels in same manner.

Fig. B

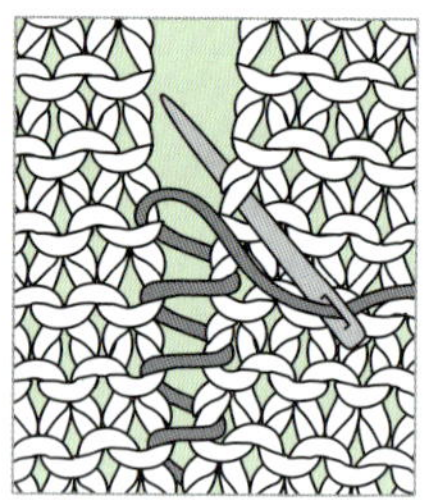

FRINGE

Holding 4 strands of yarn, each 16" (40.5 cm) long, add fringe to every other stitch across short edges of Afghan ***(Figs. 8a & b, page 30)***, matching colors.

Sweet Baby's Blanky

Finished Size: 38" (96.5 cm) square

EASY

Instructions continued on page 24.

SHOPPING LIST

Yarn (Medium Weight) MEDIUM 4

[4 ounces, 256 yards
(113 grams, 187 meters)
per skein]:

- ☐ 4 skeins

Knitting Needle

29" (74 cm) circular

- ☐ Size 11 (8 mm)
  or size needed for gauge

Additional Supplies

- ☐ Markers - 2

GAUGE INFORMATION

In Garter Stitch (knit every row),
12 sts = 4" (10 cm)

Note: Circular needle is used to accommodate large numbers of stitches. Do not join; work back and forth in rows.

AFGHAN

LOWER BORDER

Cast on 116 sts.

Rows 1-10: Knit across.

BODY

Row 1: K7, place marker for side border, knit across to last 7 sts, place marker for side border, K7.

Row 2 (Right side)**:** K7, slip marker, K1, ★ YO, K3, pass first st over second and third sts just knit and off needle; repeat from ★ across to 2 sts before marker, K2, slip marker, K7.

Row 3: K7, slip marker, purl across to next marker, slip marker, K7.

Row 4: K7, slip marker, K2, ★ YO, K3, pass first st over second and third sts just knit and off needle; repeat from ★ across to one st before marker, K1, slip marker, K7.

Row 5: K7, slip marker, purl across to next marker, slip marker, K7.

Rows 6-10: Knit across.

Rows 11-155: Repeat Rows 1-10, 14 times, then repeat Rows 1-5 once **more**.

UPPER BORDER

Rows 1-10: Knit across.

Bind off all sts in **knit**.

General Information

ABBREVIATIONS

cm	centimeters
K	knit
mm	millimeters
P	purl
PSSO	pass slipped stitch over
SSK	slip, slip, knit
st(s)	stitch(es)
tog	together
YO	yarn over

KNIT TERMINOLOGY		
UNITED STATES		INTERNATIONAL
gauge	=	tension
bind off	=	cast off
yarn over (YO)	=	yarn forward (yfwd) **or** yarn around needle (yrn)

Yarn Weight Symbol & Names	LACE 0	SUPER FINE 1	FINE 2	LIGHT 3	MEDIUM 4	BULKY 5	SUPER BULKY 6
Type of Yarns in Category	Fingering, size 10 crochet thread	Sock, Fingering, Baby	Sport, Baby	DK, Light Worsted	Worsted, Afghan, Aran	Chunky, Craft, Rug	Bulky, Roving
Knit Gauge Range* in Stockinette St to 4" (10 cm)	33-40** sts	27-32 sts	23-26 sts	21-24 sts	16-20 sts	12-15 sts	6-11 sts
Advised Needle Size Range	000-1	1 to 3	3 to 5	5 to 7	7 to 9	9 to 11	11 and larger

*GUIDELINES ONLY: The chart above reflects the most commonly used gauges and needle sizes for specific yarn categories.

** Lace weight yarns are usually knitted on larger needles to create lacy openwork patterns. Accordingly, a gauge range is difficult to determine. Always follow the gauge stated in your pattern.

SYMBOLS & TERMS

★ — work instructions following ★ as many **more** times as indicated in addition to the first time.

( ) or **[ ]** — work enclosed instructions **as many** times as specified by the number immediately following **or** contains explanatory remarks.

colon (:) — the number(s) given after a colon at the end of a row or round denote(s) the number of stitches you should have on that row or round.

BEGINNER	Projects for first-time knitters using basic knit and purl stitches. Minimal shaping.
EASY	Projects using basic stitches, repetitive stitch patterns, simple color changes, and simple shaping and finishing.
INTERMEDIATE	Projects with a variety of stitches, such as basic cables and lace, simple intarsia, double-pointed needles and knitting in the round needle techniques, mid-level shaping and finishing.
EXPERIENCED	Projects using advanced techniques and stitches, such as short rows, fair isle, more intricate intarsia, cables, lace patterns, and numerous color changes.

KNITTING NEEDLES																			
U.S.	0	1	2	3	4	5	6	7	8	9	10	10½	11	13	15	17	19	35	50
U.K.	13	12	11	10	9	8	7	6	5	4	3	2	1	00	000	---	---	---	---
Metric - mm	2	2.25	2.75	3.25	3.5	3.75	4	4.5	5	5.5	6	6.5	8	9	10	12.75	15	19	25

GAUGE

Exact gauge is **essential** for proper size. Before beginning your project, make a sample swatch in the yarn and needle specified in the individual instructions. After completing the swatch, measure it, counting your stitches and rows carefully. If your swatch is larger or smaller than specified, **make another, changing needle size to get the correct gauge**. Keep trying until you find the size needles that will give you the specified gauge.

INCREASES

YARN OVERS

After a knit stitch, before a knit stitch

Bring the yarn forward **between** the needles, then back **over** the top of the right hand needle, so that it is now in position to knit the next stitch *(Fig. 1a)*.

Fig. 1a

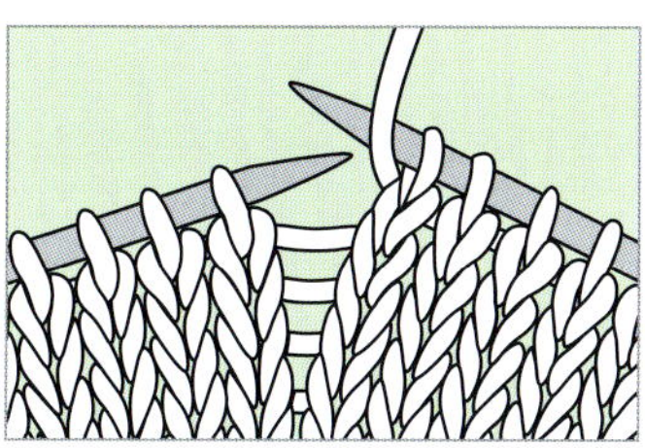

After a knit stitch, before a purl stitch

Bring the yarn forward **between** the needles, then back **over** the top of the right hand needle and forward **between** the needles again so that it is now in position to purl the next stitch *(Fig. 1b)*.

Fig. 1b

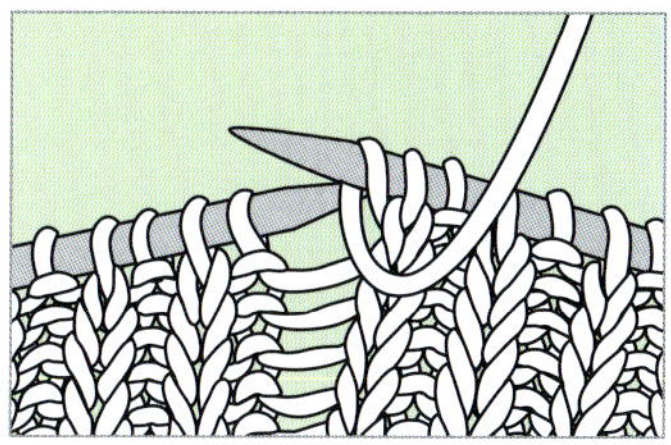

DECREASES

KNIT 2 STITCHES TOGETHER

(abbreviated K2 tog)

Insert the right needle into the front of the first two stitches on the left needle as if to **knit** *(Fig. 2)*, then knit them together as if they were one stitch.

Fig. 2

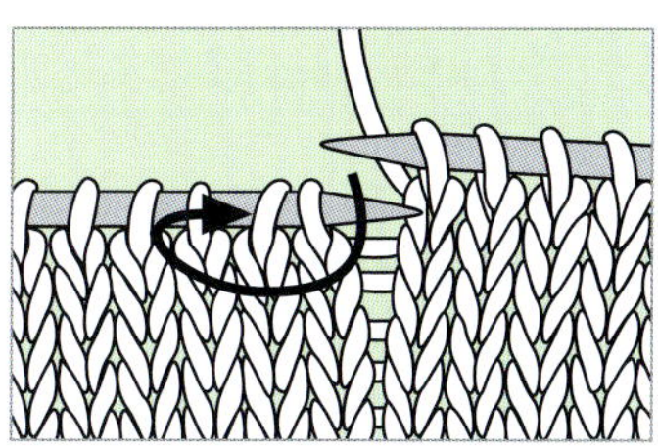

PURL 2 TOGETHER

(abbreviated P2 tog)

Insert the right needle into the **front** of the first 2 stitches on the left needle as if to **purl** *(Fig. 3)*, then **purl** them together as if they were one stitch.

Fig. 3

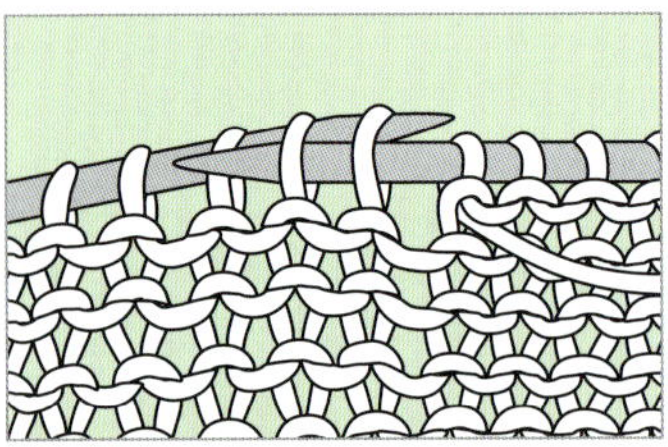

PURL 3 TOGETHER

(abbreviated P3 tog)

Insert the right needle into the **front** of the first 3 stitches on the left needle as if to **purl** *(Fig. 4)*, then **purl** them together as if they were one stitch.

Fig. 4

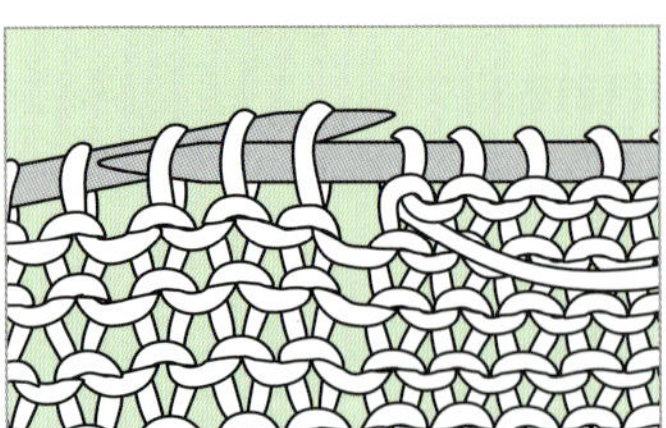

SLIP, SLIP, KNIT

(abbreviated SSK)

Separately slip two stitches as if to **knit** *(Fig. 5a)*, insert the left needle into the **front** of both slipped stitches *(Fig. 5b)*, and then knit them together as if they were one stitch *(Fig. 5c)*.

Fig. 5a

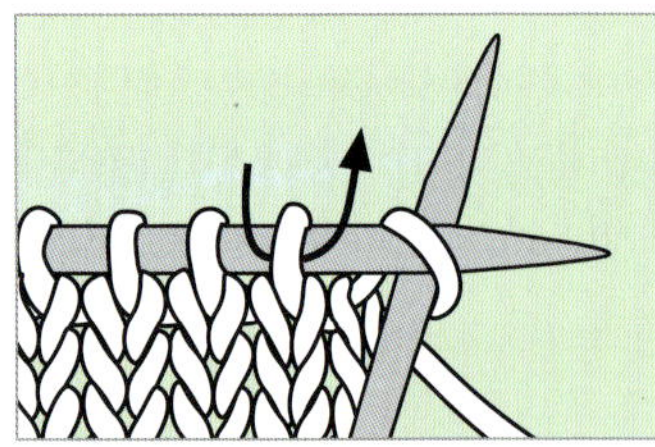

Fig. 5b

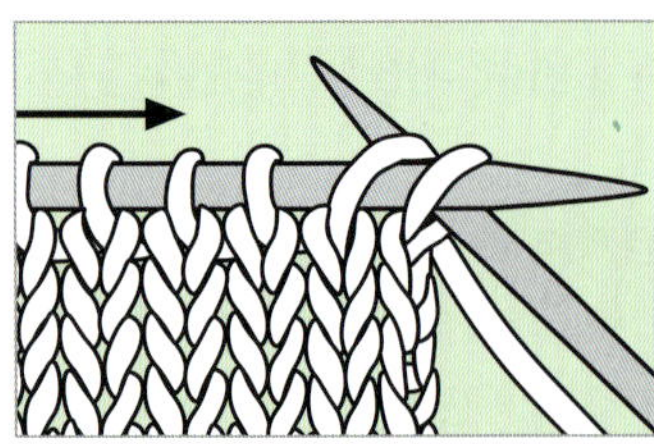

Fig. 5c

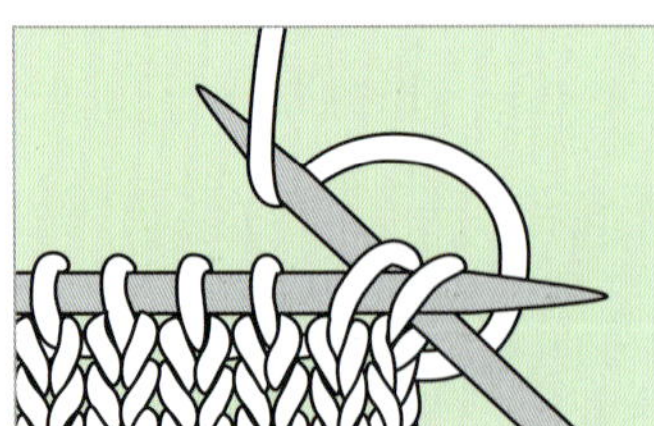

SLIP 1, KNIT 1, PASS SLIPPED STITCH OVER

(abbreviated slip 1, K1, PSSO)

Slip one stitch as if to **knit** *(Fig. 6a)*, then knit the next stitch. With the left needle, bring the slipped stitch over the knit stitch *(Fig. 6b)* and off the needle.

Fig. 6a

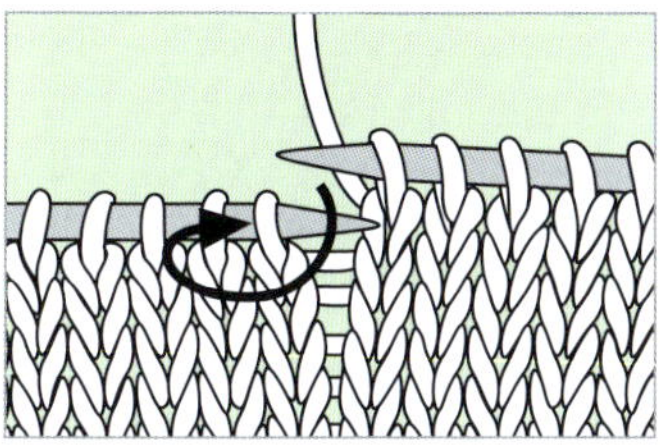

Fig. 6b

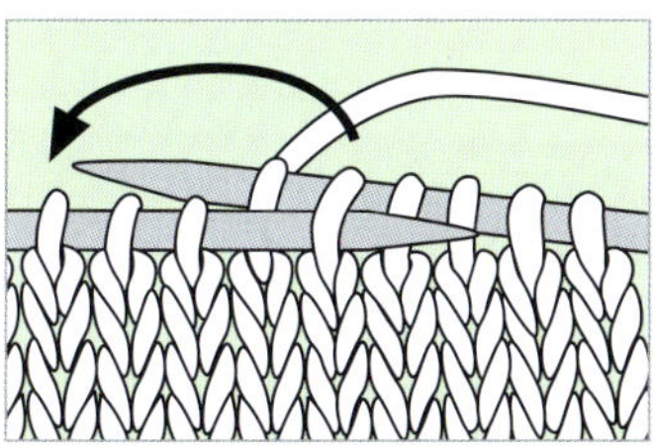

SLIP 1, KNIT 2 TOGETHER, PASS SLIPPED STITCH OVER

(abbreviated slip 1, K2 tog, PSSO)

Slip one stitch as if to **knit** *(Fig. 6a)*, then knit the next 2 stitches together *(Fig. 2, page 27)*. With the left needle, bring the slipped stitch over the stitch just made *(Fig. 7)* and off the needle.

Fig. 7

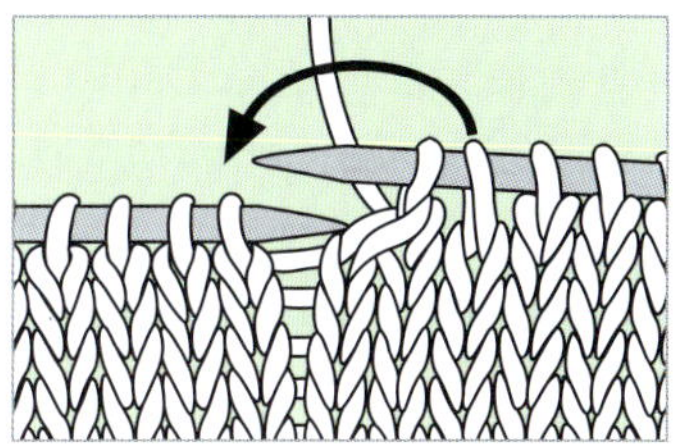

FRINGE

Cut a piece of cardboard about 6" (15 cm) wide and ½" (12 mm) longer than the length specified in the instructions. Wind the yarn loosely and evenly lengthwise around the cardboard. When the card is filled, cut the yarn across one end. Repeat as needed. Hold the specified number of strands for one fringe together, then fold in half.

Hold the project with the wrong side facing you. Using a crochet hook, draw the folded end through the space or stitch *(Fig. 8a)*. Pull the loose ends through the folded end; draw the knot up tightly *(Fig. 8b)*. Lay flat on a hard surface and trim the ends.

Fig. 8a

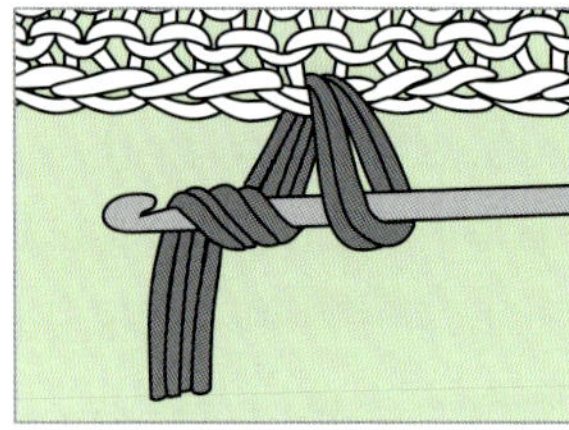

Fig. 8b

Yarn Information

Afghans in this book were made using a variety of yarn weights. Any brand of the specified weight of yarn may be used. It is best to refer to the yardage/meters when determining how many balls or skeins to purchase. Remember, to arrive at the finished size, it is the GAUGE/TENSION that is important, not the brand of yarn.

For your convenience, listed below are the specific yarns used to create our photography models. Because yarn manufacturers make frequent changes in their product lines, you may sometimes find it necessary to use a substitute yarn or to search for the discontinued product at alternate suppliers (locally or online).

LITTLE BOY BLUE
Lion Brand® Vanna's Choice® Baby
#106 Little Boy Blue

BEAUTIFUL IN GREEN SQUARED
Red Heart® Super Saver®
#672 Spring Green

LOVELY AND WARM
Red Heart® Super Saver®
#334 Buff

RHAPSODY IN RED & WHITE
Lion Brand® Homespun®
White - #300 Hepplewhite
Red - #436 Claret

RIPPLE ROMANCE
Lion Brand® Landscapes®
#204 Desert Spring

WARM AS TOAST
Lion Brand® Lion's Pride® Woolspun®
#200 Campfire Print

FISHERMAN RIPPLE
Red Heart® Super Saver®
#4313 Aran Fleck

MIDNIGHT MAGIC
Red Heart® Tweed Twist™
#9312 Neon Black

SIMPLE STRIPES
Lion Brand® Chenille
Grey - #146 Granite
Green - #130 Emerald
Variegated - #204 Multi-color

SWEET BABY BLANKY
Red Heart® Soft Baby Steps®
#746 Binky Print

We have made every effort to ensure that these instructions are accurate and complete. We cannot, however, be responsible for human error, typographical mistakes, or variations in individual work.

Afghans made and instructions tested by Kim Britt, Beth Ciaccio, Patricia Honker, Susan Lowman, and Marina Salume.

Production Team: Instructional/Technical Editor - Sarah J. Green; Editorial Writer - Susan Frantz Wiles; Senior Graphic Artist - Lora Puls; Graphic Artist - Victoria Temple; Photo Stylist - Lori Wenger; and Photographer - Jason Masters.

Produced for Leisure Arts by The Creative Partners™ LLC.